Jesus' feet

Tiffany Lee Thompson

Papa Press

Jesus' Feet by Tiffany Lee Thompson

Published by Papa Press

Publishing services provided by Pedernales Publishing, LLC
www.pedernalespublishing.com

Library of Congress Control Number: 2013910937

ISBN Number: 978-0-615-83201-2 Paperback Edition

*D*early Loved Child of God,

There are many truths told throughout Scripture about Jesus' feet. One of my favorites is found in Luke 10:38-42:

"While Jesus and His followers were traveling, Jesus went into a town. A woman named Martha let Jesus stay at her house. Martha had a sister named Mary, who was sitting at Jesus' feet and listening to Him teach. But Martha was busy with all the work to be done. She went in and said, 'Lord, don't you care that my sister has left me alone to do all the work? Tell her to help me.'

"But the Lord answered her, 'Martha, Martha, you are worried and upset about many things. Only one thing is important. Mary has chosen the better thing, and it will never be taken away from her.'"[1]

As you choose to take time to sit at Jesus' feet with me and learn from Him, may we hear Him say to us that we have chosen the only thing that is important and it will never be taken away from us! Let's look at Jesus' feet as closely as we look at a newborn baby's feet. We want to count all ten of His toes and worship with wonder the gift that we've been given in Jesus.

Sincerely Seeking Jesus' Feet,

Princess Tiffany Lee Thompson

Daughter of the Most High King of kings

This book is dedicated as worship to the Trinity: God who created me and gifted me with so many words and an opportunity to use them for encouraging His children; Jesus, my Savior, who lived a perfect life of love that inspires me to follow in His footsteps; and Holy Spirit, who gives the power to make it possible!

Acknowledgements

I've met so many amazing people in my travels, speaking. Many of them asked for a book, and here it is! It definitely wouldn't be here without God's persistence in so many different ways, including an eye twitch that wouldn't quit until I started the book. After the obedience, came the rejection by publishers and a lot of questioning (why write a book that nobody will read?) It sat on a shelf for six years. Then…people started asking about it again.

There were several people who encouraged me to try again. Thank you, Tessa Thompson, for the encouragement and endorsement. Thank you to my baby brother Justin who lives out redemption and his precious daughter, Rosie, for sharing your modeling skills for the front cover photo. Thank you, Mavericks, for all your prayers. Thank you, Jeanne Juve, for believing in me. Thank you,

Jill Briscoe, for reading it and for endorsing it. Thank you, Jose Ramirez and Barbara Rainess at Pedernales Publishing for all the time, wisdom and work that is making this dream come true. Thank you, Sue Jorgenson, for editing it.

Thank you, Mr. Amazing Timothy Thompson, for always being the wind beneath my wings. Gratefully, I don't know who I'd be without you. You have consistently cheered me on and countered all my self-doubts with God-sized faith! I praise our Papa for the gift of you and count it my biggest blessing to be your bride.

And finally, thank You, Papa God, for trusting me to encourage Your precious people. Thank you for the promise that Your word will not return to You void! I believe You and pray a blessing for all the people who will read this book. May they encounter Your great love as they sit at Jesus' feet.

Gratefully,

Tiffany Lee Thompson

Jesus' Feet

tiny feet

1

tiny feet

I have always had an active imagination, and have been easily excited. Often, I have had expectations that could never have been realized on earth. It's probably pretty normal, since we were all created to hunger for heaven. We desire a place of peace that we will not know until God takes us home.

For as long as I can remember, I wanted to be a Mommy. I loved to play with dolls. I named them, and loved to rock them to sleep. Determined at the age of five that this was God's design for me, and that He was able to give me the desires of my heart, I decided that the pretend baby dolls just weren't cutting it anymore. I wanted a real baby.

Pregnant women suddenly caught my rapt attention. It wasn't long before I asked my Mom the dreaded question, "How do you get a baby in your tummy?" I remember clearly her answer. "Well…(a long pause) a woman decides that she wants to have a baby and then she goes about having one." She looked closely at me to see if I understood. She looked very serious. The words she chose to share with me seemed wise and since she had been pregnant and had two babies by this time in her life, I understood that she knew what she was talking about.

I thanked her for all of this important information and promptly ran upstairs to get pregnant. I pulled the footstool in front of the bathroom mirror and climbed up on it to look myself straight in the eye. With the most serious voice that I could muster at the age of five, I said, "I am deciding to have a baby." I climbed off the stool and ran to my bedroom so excited.

The next step was vaguely unclear to me. Now, I needed to go about having a baby. The only thing I could think of was that I had to start "eating for two." Soon my belly would grow and then there would be a baby. I told all of my dolls a real baby would be coming soon and that I was pregnant. I would wait to tell everyone else until after I was showing…I thought that was how it was usually done.

Sleep was hard to come by, being so excited and all. Wouldn't my parents and friends be surprised? I imagined what my baby would look like. Would it be a boy or a girl? Then I realized that I would have to come up with the perfect name. Should I name the baby after someone or should the baby have a name that nobody had ever had before? Should the baby have a name from the Bible? My brother had a Biblical name, but I didn't. He didn't seem any more Godly than I was, but perhaps it was because he was only three years old.

I was tired the next morning as I got ready for kindergarten, but that was to be expected when one was expecting. It was hard to ride the bus with all my friends and keep this secret. All morning at school, I felt so special having a baby in my belly and that nobody else knew about it. I tried to hide that "glow" from the other children, because I didn't know how I would respond if they asked if I was pregnant. I knew that it was wrong to lie, but I didn't want them to know before my family knew. This is the predicament of many pregnant women. Thankfully, nobody asked me.

The morning seemed to last forever. I reminded myself on the bus ride home that I must re-member to eat for two. This was something that would not go unnoticed because mealtime was often a struggle for me. Part of the problem was that good manners were highly esteemed in our family. An important part of that was not talking with your mouth full. Since talking was something that I spent a lot of time doing, there wasn't much time to have food in my mouth during a meal. Most of my eating took place after everyone else had left the table. Then there was nobody to talk to and just cold food left on my plate to be eaten.

The increase in my appetite caused my Mom to sit in shock at the table because a full mouth prevented me from talking. She almost fell off her chair when I asked for seconds. I was pretty sure that she would know that I was pregnant before I was showing because my Mom was pretty sharp. She did make a lot of comments about how well I was eating. I kept my secret and many days - probably two - went by before I noticed that I was "showing." I remember the night that I changed into my pajamas and noticed a line on my belly from where the elastic from my underpants was getting tight. I figured it was time to tell my parents.

That night when my Mom came to tuck me into bed I was smiling as wide as the sky. She asked me what I was smiling about and I said that I had a very special secret to tell her. I can still remember the surprised look on her face when I whispered that I was pregnant.

My joy bubble burst when she laughed out loud at my news and told me that it wasn't possible. Then she sat on my bed and explained that I couldn't have a baby until I was married. Oh, how my heart broke that night. I wonder if anyone ever told Mary that? It wasn't until almost two decades later when I actually married, decided to have a baby and then went about having one.

When my first child was born, I wept with wonder. I honestly thought that my dreams and expectations were beyond being beat, but hands down, beyond a shadow of a doubt, the joy of finally being a Mommy blew me away! The love that flooded my soul surprised me. This tiny baby in my arms almost made my heart explode. I knew that I would give my life to spare her any pain.

The love that I had for my child was so intense and in an instant, my relationship with God was changed forever. It was a sudden shock to realize what love He has for me when He calls me His child. The unbelievable revelation that He loved me as much or more than I loved this baby in my arms absolutely undid me.

You are His precious child as well. He loves you. Can we believe that God holds us in His arms and just weeps over the gift that we are to Him? Does He marvel at every tiny thing about us? Yes, He does. He loves us more than we love our children. He knows how many hairs are on our head. I was so in awe of my real baby, but I did not count the hairs on her head, and there really weren't that many.

Everything about my baby amazed me, especially her tiny feet. I kissed her feet and put her tiny toes in my mouth and I can tell you that was something that I had never done to anyone else before. She was so pure and sweet and innocent and small. The wonder of it all is that Almighty God sent His Son to earth as a baby. Jesus had tiny feet too.

Sometimes when I read God's truths, my mind is blown away. Have you pondered the proportionate truth of this verse found in Isaiah 66:1? "This is what the LORD says: 'Heaven is My throne and the earth is My footstool.'" [1] Can you comprehend how gigantic His feet must be? The distance from America to Africa may only be the breadth of His big toe. No wonder He is omnipresent. He is everywhere at once because He is huge!

When I ponder again the amazing gift of baby Jesus, my sense of wonder increases as I consider the miracle of His tiny feet. How can a God that is so big become so small? How can feet that dance beyond the stars become so humble as to lie in the hay? How does the Holy Perfect Alpha and Omega fit into a baby? As angels sing at Christmastime about the newborn King, I wrestle again to grasp the humility of our Great God.

The only answer that I can come up with is love. Love so great that it is willing to be a baby. It's mind-bending, soul-shattering and beyond belief love. Oh, how He loves you and me! Don't you just love Jesus' tiny feet?

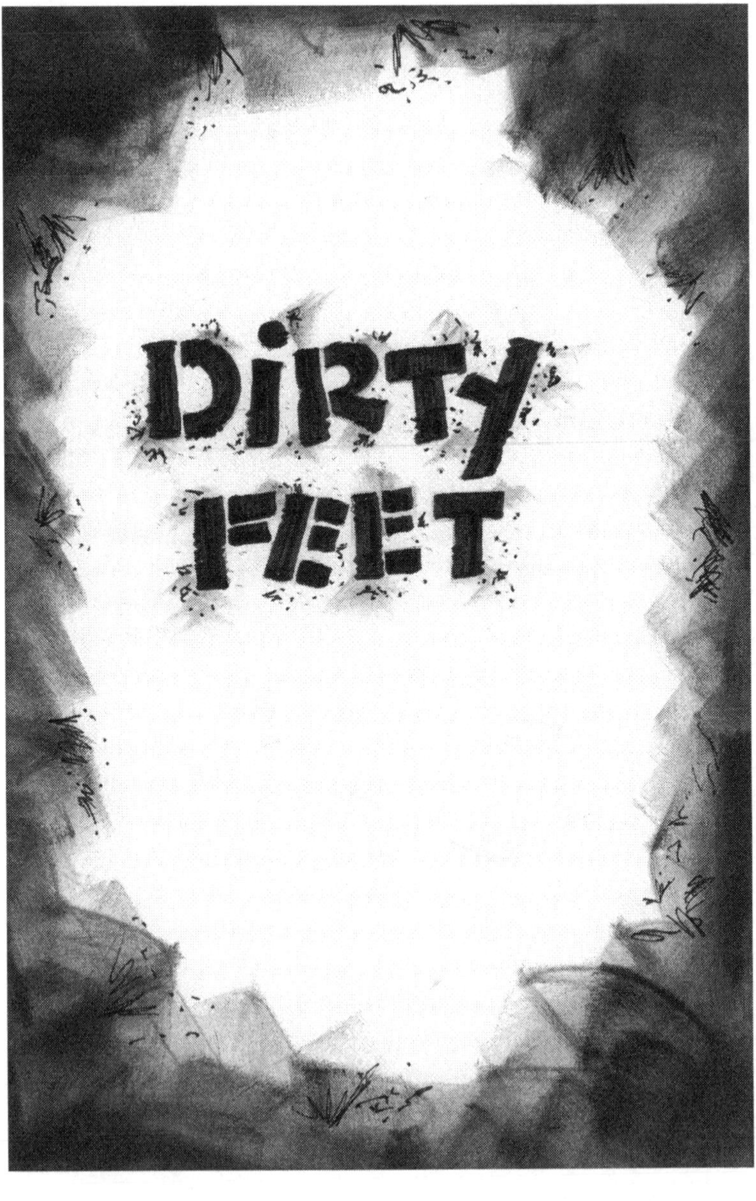
DIRTY
FEET

2
dirty feet

*J*esus was a little boy. In other words, He was a hungry noise with dirt on Him. Can you even conceive of this?

JESUS WAS HUNGRY

As I think about it a bit, I think I might be hungry right now too. Does that make me Godly? Does it affect you this way? Wouldn't it be funny if you loaned this book to a friend and it was returned with chocolate smudges on this page?

Think about God who provides everything for us. I mean, at the dinner table it is always God whom we thank for the food, because even though I make the dinner, I don't *make* the food, such as the chicken, the lettuce, etc.

God was a little boy asking for something to eat. Have you wondered if He ever ate something He didn't like? Do you think that they have food in heaven? I have always thought that there must be great food in heaven and you could eat as much of it as you like and never get fat. The calories wouldn't count. Someone say Hallelujah! Aren't you excited that you are invited to spend eternity there? It is so amazing to spend time with Jesus now; as invisible as He is, I simply squeal inside when I think of seeing Him face to face!

Jesus was needy. That just freaks me out, because I know that He is the only one who can meet all of my needs. He humbled Himself to be like me. He wants me to know that it's okay to be needy. The creation of our appetites and our need for food so often in a day is an analogy of our need for God. To know that He had to eat and drink when He Himself is the bread of life and living water is a difficult concept to grasp.

We are often afraid to admit our needs. It is hard to be needy and we try to convince ourselves that we are self-sufficient. But Jesus didn't do that. "He was hungry." [1] Mary and Martha each saw that Jesus was hungry. One saw the need to feed Him physically with food and the other saw with eyes attuned to His spiritual hunger. Mary saw that Jesus was hungry for her heart. What are you particularly hungry for? Are you hungry for healthy relationships? We know that this hunger is part of our likeness to Christ.

Jesus was hungry for people to know truth and to live truth. He was hungry for us to love and to know that we are loved, loved beyond our wildest imaginations. He was hungry for us to love Him, to know Him, to trust Him. Isn't trust love in action? Sometimes love can sound like a Valentine's Day card or a sweet feeling. But love is action. It is more than a feeling or an emotion; it's a verb, it's a noun, it's a mystery and it's what we are most hungry for. "God is love." [2] We are hungry for God. I think that God is hungry for us too.

JESUS WAS NOISE

This popular description of little boys includes noise. Do you have any boys in your family? Can you relate to this? The noise is just loud. It's hard for me to picture Jesus like this. I think of God having a still small voice. I also think of all the sweet, serene pictures that I see of Jesus yet I can hardly picture Him talking. There are a lot of red letters in my Bible to prove that He had important things to say. He learned how to talk. He said adorable things when He was two years old. And like other boys He probably made a lot of noise. He probably growled like a bear, and I would assume that since He created the bear's growl, it would have been very impressive. He might have even scared His mother and His friends.

It surprises me to realize all the little categories and boxes that I put God in. I have a hundred different voices. The soft cooing of a dove that I used for speaking to my newborn baby and the screeching, warning voice as my two-year-old ran toward the street to fetch a ball. I have my happy answer-the-phone voice and all the crazy, endless hours of blah, blah, blah when I get my hair done, because it is incredibly un-comfortable to have someone play with my hair that long without talking. If I am capable of dif-ferent volumes and inflections in my voice, if I can communicate much just by the tone of my voice, can't God do the same?

One frustration about writing instead of talking is that the spirit behind the words is not audibly heard. I pray that you will have the gift of dis-cernment as you read this to hear the humor and laughter, reverence and worship, hope and encouragement, passion, tears and all of that. We are emotional people. We are created in the image of God, and God is emotional. There is evidence of it everywhere. Can you imagine His laugh? Can you see Him cry? Do you feel His anger as He floods the earth? Do you see His humility and vulnerability as He comes to earth for you and me in the cloak of humanity? Can you see His frustration as He tells us the truth and we don't get it? Communication is a sticky thing, because it is always a two-way street.

Consider all the ways that this phrase could be interpreted: "You are looking hot tonight." Does that mean that your face is flushed and there are large rings of sweat under your armpits? Does that mean that you are dressed inappropriately, perhaps wearing a turtleneck and earmuffs when it is 65 degrees outside? (I just realized that if you live in the South, you would not understand why I picked that temperature, but that could be a summer day in Wisconsin.) Does it mean that you are looking so sexy? This last thought is probably the only one that came to mind, right?

I assume that like me, you have different ways of interpreting what is said; my concern in writing this book is that you might not understand what I am saying. I am not God. (Not that you mistook me for Him.) God is perfect and tells us the truth perfectly, but our interpretation is often inaccurate, so how much more likely it is for the message here to be missed. It feels like an enormous responsibility. Maybe you have something in your life like that right now. There is something that God is laying on your heart, but you are afraid that your inadequacies will mess it up. Is there someone on your heart that God is asking you to share the gospel with? Is there someone in your life from whom you're estranged and God is asking you to address it? Is there some sin in your life that God continues to ask you to forsake, but you just don't have the ability to forsake it? Whatever it is...do it! Our lives here are short and they are meant to be purposeful. "Do whatever He tells you." [3]

What is He telling you? Jesus was noise. He spoke. He still speaks. He says a lot of important things, the most important things. His words are precious. His Word is eternal. Have you heard Him speak lately?

Living in Wisconsin, I don't often get to hear the ocean or the roar of waterfalls...okay, almost never. But recently I was in Mexico by the Pacific Ocean. (I know, lucky me.) I was just amazed by the soothing sound of the rushing waves crashing on the shore. I could sit on the shore with my eyes closed and listen to it for hours and at night I left the window open so that it would sing me to sleep. It was a wonderful sound, but even more so after reading Revelation 1:15: "...His voice was like the sound of rushing waters." [4] It makes perfect sense to me that the voice of God would be that soothing and that powerful and that constant. There is no language in which He can't be heard. God speaks every language and so often He is speaking without words. He is amazing! I believe that He is speaking all the time; we could hear Him if we would just take the time to listen. Listening to an invisible God is difficult...but there is nothing else more worth the effort. Schedule time to listen to Him. Psalm 46:10 is a challenging verse for me in every version that I have read because it's hard for me to be still.

"Be still, and know that I am God." NIV [5]

"Cease striving and know that I am God." NAS [6]

"Be quiet and know that I am God." NCV [7]

"Step out of the traffic! Take a long, loving look at Me, your High God." MSG [8]

Let us take the time to listen to the noise of

God...the voice that spoke us into being, the gurgle of a newborn baby, and the first words of a baby boy. Imagine the Great I AM who spoke the world into existence learning how to say "Please," and imagine Him saying, "Mama, I wuv ooo," and how those words must have melted Mary's heart as those words from the mouths of our own flesh and blood melt ours. And now, will you hear the tender voice of God as a child looking up at you with sheer innocence and humility say "I wuv ooo"? Let us hear all the truths He spoke to teach us about life and love as well as anticipate the words we will hear in heaven. Oh, how I long to hear Him say, "Well done, good and faithful servant." [9]

JESUS WAS DIRTY

Can you imagine the hands that formed the universe and fashioned your face reaching up to you to be held? Can we begin to believe how enormous the love of God is to humble Himself to be a boy with dirty feet?

Last summer I had the privilege of being part of a mission trip to Haiti, the poorest country in the Western Hemisphere. One day while I was walking alone on a dirt road, I saw a thin boy in rags, about eight years old, walking barefoot and coaxing a skinny donkey loaded down with full burlap sacks. Suddenly I was struck with the reality that Jesus had been a boy. He had lived in a culture without the comforts that I have. I was really uncomfortable there, with warm water to drink and no air conditioning, lots of dirt and bad smells, mostly coming from my own body; there was no running water or showers to speak of. It was a giant culture shock for me, and I remember reading 1 Peter while I was there and pondering the suffering I was going through. But when I saw that boy, I began to cry. What kind of culture shock did Jesus go through to come to earth from heaven? I had always read about Jesus' suffering and thought of the cross. I hadn't even thought of the whole thirty-three years that He walked the earth as a long mission trip; a huge sacrifice; a humble gift; and a beautiful way to say I love you.

How many feet has God created? I can't comprehend all the people's feet created by Him. He, who created legs and feet, learned to walk. He, who spoke the universe into existence, learned to talk. He, who provides us with nourishment, was Himself hungry. Jesus was a little boy. Jesus was a hungry noise with dirt on Him. Jesus had dirty feet.

Jesus' feet

3
Dancing Feet

*H*ave you ever read God's word and a verse just jumped off the page at you? Sometimes I find myself catching my breath because the truth is startling or so beautiful. There is a verse found in Zephaniah 3 which says, "The LORD your God is with you, He is mighty to save. He will take great delight in you, He will quiet you with His love, He will rejoice over you with singing." [1]

Did that make you catch your breath? Have you read that before? Do you believe it? Isn't that an amazing news flash? As I ponder all of its meaning, I am astounded again that the God of the universe and of all creation cares for me, protects me, delights in me, and dances over me. The description of Him rejoicing over me is best described by dancing, specifically leaping for joy and even twirling. And doesn't the orbit of our entire galaxy make more sense when we consider our Great God twirling? Of course we would all be spinning in the wind that He creates.

The idea of God dancing and singing is such a switch from the God that I have spent much of my life hearing about in church. It is incredible to me that I have spent decades believing that I blessed Him with my songs of worship and how little time I ever gave to listening to His song for me. And as far as the dancing, how could I keep from dancing if I heard His song? I was taught that Christians aren't supposed to dance.

I attended a Christian college that actually had students sign a contract agreeing not to do such "sinful" things. This sort of thinking is how Christians get the label the *frozen chosen*. It is sad to think that we who bear Christ's name and are the dwelling place of His Holy Spirit could be so dull. We have a dancing God! We have a joyful God! Jesus was oozing with the fruit of the Spirit and that means that He was the most joyful human ever.

Jesus came to this earth to be our example of who we were created to be. We learn so much from studying Him. Jesus went to a wedding. Can you picture Him standing quietly in the back waiting to perform a miracle? When I ask myself these kinds of questions, I am sad to answer honestly and then see what I really believe about Jesus. When I ponder it, I realize that Jesus would never have been a distant, un-involved observer. He knew that the number of breaths He had on earth were few. He knew that He was there for a purpose and I think that He lived every moment completely aware of all the eternal implications of it. He had an absolutely pure heart of God. He would have celebrated love more than any other person there at the wedding.

I believe that Jesus was the first to hit the dance floor. He danced with an abandonment that we will never know, because we are always wondering what other people think of us. He never had to wonder because He knew. What's even better, He really didn't care. He wasn't trying to impress anyone. Jesus lived for an audience of One, for the glory of His Father. He probably felt limited by gravity during His dance. He may have felt as though it was His least spectacular dance, but I believe that it had to be the most beautiful dance that anyone on earth had ever seen.

Jesus celebrated life! Jesus turned water into wine! That makes a lot of people really uncomfortable. It doesn't say that He drank the wine, or that He turned all the wine into water. Some people say that the wine in Biblical times was different from wine today; it was more like grape juice. When I buy grape juice (notice that I didn't say that I buy wine), it is full of preservatives to keep it from fermenting.

Please consider a couple of questions. Do you think there were a lot of preservatives in Biblical times? Do you think that there was much refrigeration? And then there is the interesting information found in John 2:9-11: "And when the headwaiter tasted the water which had become wine, and did not know where it came from (but the servant who had drawn the water knew) the headwaiter called the bridegroom, and said to him, 'Every man serves the good wine first, and when men have drunk freely, then that which is poorer; you have kept the good wine until now.' This beginning of His signs Jesus did in Cana of Galilee, and manifested His glory, and His disciples believed in Him."[2]

Wine and dancing seem to go together. A few years ago my husband, Timothy, and I took dancing lessons. It was a wonderful four weeks of date nights. Tim made it clear that we would not be continuing with the lessons. He pointed out that his tennis shoes were wider across than the instructor's shoes were lengthwise. He thought that maybe he didn't really have "dancing feet." The instructor was quick to affirm my man's coordination and sense of rhythm but that he might benefit from a bottle of wine to loosen up a bit. We all laughed and thought that a bottle of wine might mess up the other two things he had going for him.

The truth is that Tim does have dancing feet. He was born with them. We have a video that his parents took of him when he was just a couple of months old. He is grinning from ear to ear looking at his adoring parents, and his feet are moving so fast that they are just a blur. Have you seen babies do this? Can't you just feel their excitement? When was the last time you were that excited? I believe that there are still reasons to get that excited. I am excited about you falling in love with Jesus as we sit as His feet. Let's toast to that with just one more glass of wine.

This year my New Year's resolution was to be drunk in the Spirit. Ephesians 5:18 says, "Do not be drunk with wine, which will ruin you, but be filled with the Spirit." [3] I think that the analogy is excellent, not that God's word would be anything other than excellent. My eight-year-old son asked me to explain my resolution to him. I explained it like this: there is a normal way to drive. It involves staying in your own lane and following the rules of the road. It is illegal to drive when you are drunk because you begin to break the rules. It's dangerous. An officer would pull someone over who was weaving in and out of his or her own lane or who seemed out of control and test them for drunk driving.

I want my life to look like that. I want others to notice that I am out of control. I want to be under the influence of the Spirit. I want to weave out of my own lane, my own agenda and interests, and let my life influence other people.

Obviously, I want that to be a more positive influence than that of a drunk driver.

I believe that Jesus had dancing feet. I believe that He celebrated love and was excited about what the Spirit of God was up to. Jesus was not inhibited in any way. He was emotionally involved. He surprised and irritated a lot of religious people. Luke 7:33-34 says, "John the Baptist came and did not eat bread or drink wine, and you say, 'He has a demon in him.' The Son of Man has come eating and drinking, and you say, 'Look at Him! He eats too much and drinks too much wine, and He is a friend of tax collectors and sinners!'" [4] It sounds like Jesus was breaking a lot of rules and weaving into the wrong lanes. I think He was drunk in the Spirit, dancing the destiny that His Creator had called Him to. This is also our example and our destiny.

Jesus, thank You for being joyful! Thank You for loving us and inviting us to celebrate love with You. We want to feel Your tender embrace as we follow Your dancing feet.

OBEDIENT FEET

4
Obedient Feet

*T*oday, I don't want to write. I would rather be on the phone or out shopping. It would be much more fun to be out for lunch with a friend, sharing some great conversation. This feels so one-sided. I write and no one responds. It's lonely. If I am to be alone, it seems that I should at least accomplish something on this long list of things I need to get done. There are flowers to plant and laundry piled knee-deep to wash. There is a pail of paint that I bought months ago to paint the girls' room, but all I have done with it is stub my toes on it.

People and projects both appear to be far more purposeful than sitting here scribbling words on a piece of paper that I have no assurance of ever being published or read by anyone. But today, it is an obedience thing. God has told me in so many wild ways that He wants me to write this book, and today I am obeying. So many days, I tell Him He's crazy (I think He gets that a lot). The joking quickly turns to wrestling and who in their right mind really wants to wrestle with God? He's bigger, He's stronger, and He's smarter. It seems such a strange thing that anyone would dare to take Him on, but humanity does it regularly. Why?

I find one reason is because our perception of pain and pleasure is bigger than our perception of God and His purposes. I see God asking me to give up my agenda, which is simply to avoid pain and embrace pleasure. Today I want to experience laughter and great conversation with friends. This conversation would very likely even be about Him, but sometimes, I would rather talk about how awesome God is than really serve Him or surrender my agenda to Him. I argue that I don't want to be home alone, but truly, because He is always with me, I am never alone.

If I accomplish a task that I choose, it would be something noticeable, like painting a room a different color or having clean clothes in the drawers. It all comes down to what will serve my agenda, instead of serving Him and trusting His agenda, which is not yet revealed by Him. That is just irritating, isn't it?

I am not Jesus. You know that, and I know that, but He lives inside of me. He calls me His friend and He sets an example for me. Whenever I look at Jesus, I fall more and more in love with Him. Jesus has obedient feet. He tells us in John 6:38, "I came down from heaven not to follow my own whim but to accomplish the will of the One who sent me."[1] Well, I guess we shouldn't be surprised.

This can inspire us, but He was, after all, fully

God and fully man. "The Son is the radiance of God's glory and the exact representation of His being." [2] He never sinned. That's exactly why His time in Gethsemane makes me fall more in love with Him. He wrestled with God. He didn't want to feel pain. He didn't walk into betrayal, false accusations, injustice, torture, humiliation and crucifixion lightly. He didn't just whistle some spiritual tune called "God's will be done." It was a sacrifice that cost Him His life. God was asking a lot. He usually does and it usually costs us something. The price of obedience is our time, our pride, and an adjustment in our priorities.

Let's go to the Garden of Gethsemane in our imaginations. Have you ever been there in real life? I haven't, but I want to go there someday. I will have to use my imagination for now. I see Jesus there, heavy-hearted and asking His friends to come with Him. It is dark and quiet in the garden. He is humble in asking His friends to pray with Him. Do you ask your friends to pray with you?

He goes further still to be alone with His God. Our prayers are different when we're alone with God than when we're with others. He cries out to God with an honest heart. He is without sin; still He struggles with anticipating pain. The sacrifice of His obedience increases in my eyes. He was human. He had feelings that would hurt from betrayal. He had nerve endings that would hurt when He was beaten. Jesus had flesh that would bleed when He was whipped. He had emotions, which He expressed in fervent prayer.

Fervent, honest prayer will do our souls good and make a difference in the world. James says, "The prayer of a righteous person is powerful and effective." [3] This scripture has never encouraged me because I don't really consider myself righteous. But because of the cross, we are forgiven and considered righteous in God's sight. If we read it correctly, the fervent prayer of a forgiven person is powerful and effective. In that case, I am *really* encouraged to pray.

Jesus cries out to His Abba. Abba is a child's name for father. It suggests dependence and such a sweet innocence and helplessness from Jesus. It also implies a trust in one whom is bigger, stronger, and wiser and who has His best interests at heart.

In John's account, an angel came to strengthen Him when His sweat fell to the ground like drops of blood. Maybe He was envisioning His blood dropping to the ground as His sweat did. I would have been freaking out! I'm glad an angel came to strengthen Him, and amazed that He needed it. I am also amazed that I don't anticipate that God would do the same for me. I'm certainly weaker than Jesus was! I need to be strengthened. Too often I do self-strengthening talks, like "It's not that bad," or 'It'll be okay," or "It's not the end of the world," but Jesus didn't talk Himself out of His emotions. He fervently took them to His Father.

And God didn't change His mind. How arrogant I am sometimes to think God will give up or go away if I don't acknowledge Him or that He will change His mind if I whine enough. He is a wise and relentless God and deep down I love that about Him. However, I don't always live my life from deep within. Often I'm shallow and easily annoyed. I roll my eyes at God's assignments, reminding Him of how busy I am or how His plan doesn't really make much sense to me.

Oh, Father, forgive me again and thank You for Jesus, Your adored Son who was real about acknowledging how much Your assignment would cost Him and surrendered enough to obey anyway. His sacrifice has saved me. May

I be willing to trust you, to obey all You ask of me regardless of the cost. May I remember it's not all about me. You have so many children to set free. Speak Your truth through me. Make me a light to dispel the darkness. Thank You for every opportunity to make a difference in eternity.

Where would we be without Jesus' obedient feet?

Jesus' Feet

Wet feet

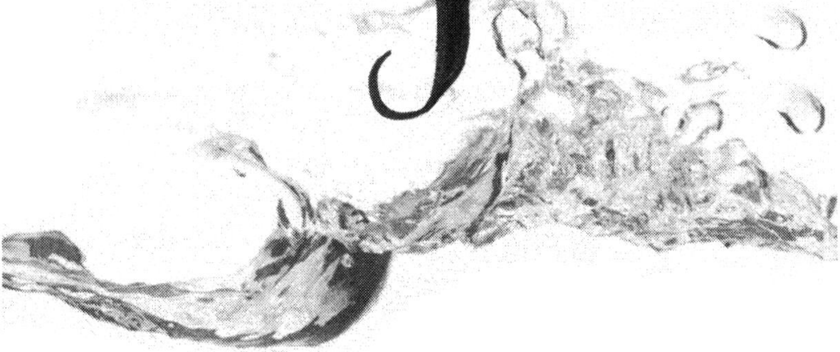

5
Wet Feet

The story of Jesus walking on the water, found in Matthew 14:22-31, is one of my favorite stories in the Bible.

"Immediately Jesus made the disciples get into the boat and go on ahead of Him to the other side, while He dismissed the crowd. After He had dismissed them, He went up on a mountainside by Himself to pray. Later that night, He was there alone, and the boat was already a considerable distance from land, buffeted by the waves because the wind was against it. Shortly before dawn Jesus went out to them, walking on the lake. When the disciples saw Him walking on the lake, they were terrified. 'It's a ghost,' they said, and cried out in fear."

"But Jesus immediately said to them: 'Take courage! It is I. Don't be afraid.'

"'Lord, if it's You,' Peter replied, 'tell me to come to You on the water.'

"'Come,' He said.

"Then Peter got down out of the boat, walked on the water and came toward Jesus. But when he saw the wind, he was afraid and, beginning to sink, cried out, 'Lord, save me!'

"Immediately Jesus reached out His hand and caught him. 'You of little faith,' He said, 'why did you doubt?'"[1]

I would like to think that Jesus was showing off, but I am sure that He was always shielding us from the splendor and power that belonged to Him. Maybe He was lost in prayer and just began walking calmly in the direction of His disciples and wasn't especially aware that He was walking on the water. Perhaps He was surprised by the disciples' fear when they saw Him. He had spent so much time with them, and they had recognized Him so many times. He had never been mistaken for a ghost, not even at the transfiguration.

I am not sure with whom you identify in the story, but I always want to be Peter, jumping out of the boat with abandon and deep faith that he could do what Jesus did. He wanted to be with Jesus walking on the water. And I have wanted that too. I have even passionately prayed for it, and yet so many days I sit like the other disciples in the boat, watching someone else walk on the water. I think that Jesus should choose someone else: someone braver, or smarter than I am. I assume that He is talking to someone else when He says, "Follow Me."

And viewing the events from the boat, the one

walking on the water with Jesus really looks amazing. From the boat, I may be jealous. I say things like, "Wow, Jesus really loves them, doesn't He?" Inside I might say, "I wish Jesus loved me like that," or "I wish that He would pick me." I love the fact that Peter didn't have it all together, that even in the middle of an extraordinary and amazing miracle something went wrong. He messed up. This is the story of my life, and I just love that I am not the only one.

Then the moment comes when I think Jesus is calling me to do something that, quite frankly, is impossible, like walking on water, and I freak! I can't sleep, I complain during my prayer time, and I try to explain to God that He has made a mistake. That looks even stranger in print than it feels in real life. I long to experience miracles in my life and then when the opportunity comes along, I am still sitting in the boat with a life preserver, shivering with self-doubt.

Jesus' Feet

I'd like to think that I am like a well-trained, perfect-attendance obedience school dog. Jesus is my master and I run to greet Him with my tail wagging. I make Him smile and I obey all of His commands. But I feel that I am much more like a cat, lying lazily around in my own little world and not even acknowledging Jesus' presence as He enters the room. He calls my name and I don't respond, let alone come. I stretch, yawn and walk away as if I don't need Him.

But I do need Him. I need Him so much more than I am even aware of. I think that I am much more aware of my need for the boat, and a life preserver in the wild water of life. But He is my all and all! I don't want a mediocre, sitting-in-the-boat kind of faith. I don't want my life to be all about my fears and insecurities. I want to trust Him more and step out into the miraculous adventure that He is capable of providing for me, when I follow Him.

When we read this story of Peter joining Jesus, walking on the water, have you wondered why all the other disciples stay in the boat? Why would anyone be a boat potato when water walking was an option? There is an amazing book titled *If You Want to Walk on Water, You've Got to Get Out of the Boat*, by John Ortberg. The chapters have questions at the end to help you process the information and to let it have an actual impact on your life. After the first chapter, the discussion questions ask, "What's your boat? Where is fear or comfort keeping you from trusting God?"[2] I remember thinking to myself, "What great questions!" And then I turned the page to start the next chapter. The Holy Spirit kept nudging me to go back and answer the questions. What if not answering them means staying in the boat? What if answering them means stepping out and experiencing a miracle? When I pushed myself to answer these questions, I didn't like the answer. It made me sad because it sounded like the sort of thing a seventh-grader would say. Certainly I must have matured more than that in all these years, but apparently not.

You want to know what it is, don't you? Well, how unfair is that? What is your answer first? I'll write it small so that maybe you won't be able to read it. Small print is like whispering. My answer was popularity. I want everyone to like me, and if I get out of the boat, someone else might get wet or offended. I live in so much fear of disappointing others. When I know that someone doesn't approve of me, I obsess about it. I spend hours pondering why, losing sleep.

There's a difference between pleasing people and loving people. It can be determined by my motives. The following verse helps me to discern if God is my first priority. Galatians 1:10 asks, "Do you think I am trying to make people accept me? No, God is the One I am trying to please. Am I trying to please people? If I still wanted to please people, I would not be a servant of Christ." [3] There it is in black and white. Yuck! I don't want to live my life like that. You are not the first person to whom I have confessed this. I shared this with a young woman who asked me to mentor her. Ironically, she is more often the one speaking profoundly into my life. I really believe that you can't out-give God. He is always able to outdo me. It has happened repeatedly in my life.

One sunny summer afternoon, I met my friend for lunch at an adorable little coffee shop. The official mentoring had started and I had read somewhere that mentors are people farther down the road who share their weaknesses with honesty. The mentor goes first so that the one being mentored sees how it is to be vulnerable. They are assured that the mentor doesn't have it all together and aren't tempted to wear a "Christian mask." So after I shared about relationships that had gone sour or were a struggle for me, revealing my frail humanity, she had some perceptive insights. "That really seems to bother you. Do you really want everyone in the world to like you?"

My answer was "Yes! I want everyone in the world to love me." She started laughing. I was shocked! "Well, that's ridiculous! You couldn't possibly keep all those relationships going. I think it's a blessing when you don't click with someone. It's one less Christmas card to send."

Her laughter seemed so healthy, and I started to see her point. And I really love this passage from Romans 12:18 that says, "If possible, so far as it depends on you, be at peace with all men."[4] I especially like two things about this verse. *If possible*, because sometimes it is impossible; the second is *so far as it depends on you*, because sometimes it depends on the other person.

If I have forgiven and loved and prayed for this person, and they are still distant or cold or angry, I can't really control that. Each of us is only responsible for our own response. It has occurred to me that someone else being distant or withdrawn might actually be a form of peace. Peace can show itself without spending tons of time together and being best buddies.

The people in the boat are not Jesus. If they are offended because I get them wet when I jump into the water to walk on the water with my Savior, then they have a problem. I am sick of sitting in the boat worrying about all the "what ifs?" The most important thing is that I see Jesus, and respond to His sweet invitation of intimacy with Him.

I have thought for many years that if everyone that I love would all jump in together, then I could jump, no problem! I am afraid of jumping alone. Have you ever held hands with a friend on the end of a dock when you know that the lake is cold and promised each other that when you reached three you would jump together? Then you count to three in unison. I have done that many times and have experienced at least three different outcomes.

1. Both our knees buckled at the last minute and we laughed at our chickenness. (Is that a word?)

2. My friend was laughing hysterically while I screamed alone and soaking wet in the cold water.

3. We jumped together, conquered our fears and bonded for life.

I don't have any memories of me ditching a friend. Doesn't that make you want to be my friend? It may have happened but I want to believe that it didn't.

It is so much easier to do anything adventurous or risky in life with a friend by your side. It's even Biblical. According to Ecclesiastes 4:9-11, "Two are better than one because they have a good return for their labor. For if either of them falls, the one will lift up his companion. But woe to the one who falls when there is not another to lift him up. Furthermore, if two lie down together they keep warm, but how can one be warm alone?"[5]

The TTV (Tiffany Thompson Version) might read like this. "Two are better than one because then I won't be lonely. If we jump in together then I won't be as afraid. But woe to you if you promise and don't deliver, because I will be wet alone. Furthermore, if I am wet and cold, you won't remain warm alone, because I will definitely splash you!"

I have spent too much of my life sitting in the boat. I have seen Jesus on the water calling to me and I have been afraid. I have watched others, like Peter, venture out on the water and have initial success and eventual failure. I have seen the fear and unwillingness of others in the boat beside me. I have asked for someone to jump with me, and nobody seems to budge at the invitation. That is because the invitations from Jesus are so individual. They are similar in that they are for our growth and others' good and they all require individual responses.

I am sick to death of this boat. Writing this book is a very lonely thing, and I have felt Jesus asking me to do this for over six years. I have just been paralyzed with all the "what ifs" and stayed in the boat. Today I have to be with Jesus. I love that He doesn't live by the rules of this world. I love that He went ahead and got in the water first and is inviting us to join Him. He won't break His promises. He is able to save us again and again. I love that He reached out and saved Peter when he was afraid. I know I will need that.

I love Jesus' wet feet!

Jesus' feet

6
Teary Feet

"When one of the Pharisees invited Jesus to have dinner with him, He went to the Pharisee's house and reclined at the table. A woman in that town who lived a sinful life learned that Jesus was eating at the Pharisee's house, so she came there with an alabaster jar of perfume. As she stood behind Him at His feet weeping, she began to wet His feet with her tears. Then she wiped them with her hair, kissed them and poured perfume on them.

"When the Pharisee who had invited Him saw this, he said to himself, 'If this Man were a prophet, He would know who is touching Him and what kind of woman she is—that she is a sinner.'

"Jesus answered him, 'Simon, I have something to tell you.'

'Tell me, Teacher,' he said.

"'Two people owed money to a certain moneylender. One owed him five hundred denarii, and the other fifty. Neither of them had the money to pay him back, so he forgave the debts of both. Now which of them will love him more?'

"Simon replied, 'I suppose the one who had the bigger debt forgiven.'

"'You have judged correctly,' Jesus said.

"Then He turned toward the woman and said to Simon, 'Do you see this woman? I came into your house. You did not give Me any water for My feet, but she wet My feet with her tears and wiped them with her hair. You did not give Me a kiss, but this woman, from the time I entered, has not stopped kissing My feet. You did not put oil on My head, but she has poured perfume on My feet. Therefore, I tell you, her many sins have been forgiven—as her great love has shown. But whoever has been forgiven little loves little.'

"Then Jesus said to her, 'Your sins are forgiven.'

"The other guests began to say among themselves, 'Who is this who even forgives sins?'

"Jesus said to the woman, 'Your faith has saved you; go in peace.'" [1]

Reading this Scripture story about Jesus' teary feet really blesses me. First of all, it is incredible to me that He was so approachable. A woman with a bad reputation, who was not invited, came in anyway and wept at Jesus' feet. She let her hair down and wiped His feet with her hair.

This was completely unacceptable in that culture. The women were not supposed to touch or even approach men, and their head and hair had to be covered. I am not sure we can even begin to understand this concept in our culture because we don't have very much that is unacceptable in our culture, since there are eating establishments where women are mostly undressed as a sort of work uniform.

The approachability to Jesus that people felt is a mystery to me, because He was Holy and perfect. I have walked with the Lord for over three decades now. I am not nearly perfect and have come to accept that this will never be the case, but my life does reflect His Presence and the sanctifying work of the Holy Spirit. I fear that my own self-righteousness has gotten in the way of being approachable. I don't have a lot of reputable "sinners" coming to me in tears, pouring out their hearts vulnerably like this lady. I shudder to think that instead of emitting an aroma of mercy and grace, I smell superior and smug. Oh, how I wish that others saw love within me. I know that this lady saw that in Jesus. She had no fear of being turned away and she was desperate to show Him her devotion and repentance and accept His forgiveness and grace, no matter what ridicule she received.

And there was definitely ridicule and criticism, not only toward her, but also toward Jesus for accepting her. Have you tasted that? I have only recently begun to believe that when others criticize, it isn't always about me. A friend told me that it doesn't matter what they think, it matters what's true. I have spent far too much energy trying to please everybody, avoiding all the accusations that could potentially hurt my feelings. I am sure that you are familiar with the childhood rhyme that says, "Sticks and stones can break my bones, but words can never hurt me." Recently my wise and wonderful fourteen-year-old daughter said that it should say, "Sticks and stones can break my bones, but words can break my heart." That makes much more sense to me.

What would it look like to be free from self-protection? What would it look like to love and worship Jesus without any hesitation? I was at a Christian music festival recently and during a worship session I began to weep. I had to confess to Jesus that there have been plenty of times that I have worshipped Him with my words and with songs, but I am still slow to bring Him my broken heart and worship Him with my tears. Why do we fight brokenness? There are so many voices in my head that tell me to pull myself together, and that's not a Bible verse in case you are wondering. It is a lie from the pit of hell! I cannot pull myself together. Instead I need to bring my broken self to Jesus. He alone is able to take all the broken pieces of my heart and put them together. This seems to be the story of my life. Maybe it makes more sense to me because my name is Tiffany.

Jesus' feet

Tiffany lamps surround me. They have been beautiful gifts from people who love me. When I look at the multi-colored pieces of broken glass and the lead that holds them together, I see a design that is beautiful, especially when the light shines through. Jesus says that He is "the light of the world."[2] He wants to shine in our lives, but our lives are like broken pieces of glass. We can bring them to Him, and lay them at His feet. Then He gets the lead out. The lead is the blood of Jesus on the cross. He paid the price for every single sin and every single mistake. He is our Redeemer. He can take all the pieces and put them into His design and make something beautiful of our lives. Jesus also said, "You are the light of the world." [3]

God treasures tears. Scripture says "You have kept count of my tossings; put my tears in your bottle." [4] This concept seems pretty contrary to our culture. We have newscasters who tell us of

67

terrible events without even a trace of emotion and it's called "professional."

Mission trips are opportunities for God to teach me amazing truths. When I was in Honduras with a team of twenty-two Americans, I heard an affirmation of tears. One morning a woman on the team woke up crying. Many people on the team asked her, "What's wrong?" She responded that she didn't know. She seemed embarrassed by her tears and the team rallied around her to pray for her and comfort her. We hugged Beth and were all very concerned for her. We went ahead with our plans for the day and left in vans for a small village where we were providing a free medical clinic for the sick and activities for the children.

When we unloaded from the vans, Beth was still crying. I was with her when a young Honduran woman came up to us. She saw Beth's tears and smiled. She reached out and gently caught a tear on her finger and held it before her as if it were a treasure. She said, "You are crying. How beautiful! God is cleansing your soul." Then she walked away. My mouth was hanging open. I could feel my brains scrambling to make sense of what had just happened. I couldn't ever remember a time in my life where I had heard tears affirmed. But the more I thought about it, the more I knew it was true.

It is amazing when you have heard lies so many times you believe them, but when you hear the truth the lies fade away. "Then you will know the truth, and the truth will set you free."[5] When I think of tears as precious proof of God cleansing souls, I worry more about not being tender enough to cry than about being tough enough that my soul is not stirred so deeply.

Since this experience, I have tried not to ask others who weep, "What's wrong?" I think the very nature of the question could suggest that it's wrong to cry. I want to thank others for trusting me with their tears. I want to affirm their feelings and explore the emotions and events that evoke their tears. Jesus didn't suggest for a moment that there was something wrong with this weeping woman at His feet. He knew that her soul was being cleansed. I believe that He saw her tears as a gift to Him. He treasured her tears. They are His way of helping us pray. "In the same way, the Spirit helps us in our weakness. We do not know what we ought to pray for, but the Spirit Himself intercedes for us through wordless groans." [6]

There have been a few times in my life when I have sobbed from the depths of my soul and found comfort in this verse, and permission to just let my tears be prayers on their own without having to put them into words. God knows our hearts and why we cry. He cares about our tears and there are unspoken prayers uttered all the time.

It turns out that the next day Beth was not crying. I almost said that she was better, but that would contradict so much of what I am learning is true. When we arrived back in the States several days later we found out that her daughter, who was only four years old, had suffered from a terrible asthma attack on the very day that Beth had been weeping. Her grandma had been staying with her and was desperately trying to get in touch with Beth by phone and email, and couldn't get through. But the Spirit of God got through to her. I believe that Beth's tears were prayers that may have saved her daughter's life.

The woman at Jesus' feet was weeping. She wanted Jesus to save her spiritual life. She was living a life she wasn't created for and Jesus did hear her desperate tears as prayers. There is no mention of her saying a word. Jesus welcomes her and He does not condemn her. He forgives her and He also defends her. Does this make you feel safe enough to go to Jesus without pretending? When we know that we are sinners, we have nothing to prove and nothing to hide. We can truly be free. It's not about us. It's about Jesus.

When we look honestly at the people who were with Jesus for dinner that night, with whom do we identify? Are we more like the weeping woman at His feet or the self-righteous man who was condemning her in his heart? Which one do you want to be? It is easy to see which one is more beautiful to Jesus, but it is hard to ask for humility. The choice is up to us. It is our responsibility. In other words, it is our ability to respond to Jesus. Let's be honest about our sins. Let's come to Him asking for forgiveness and weeping in worship that we are even allowed to draw near enough to touch Him.

Oh Lord, You are so generous with Your time. You are the most important One and yet You invite us to come sit at Your feet. You would let the tears of regret and shame from our sin stain Your feet. And as we reach down to wipe them away, You tell us that this is worship and that we are forgiven! What joy floods our souls! Thank You Jesus for loving us and listening, even when we have no words. Thank You for bidding us to come just as we are and for for-giving us. Thank You for such beautiful mercy. We love You! Please let our whole lives look like a beautiful love song sung for You!

We just love Your teary feet!

CLeaN
feet

7
CLEAN FEET

"After that, He poured water into a basin and began to wash His disciples' feet, drying them with the towel that was wrapped around Him. He came to Simon Peter, who said to Him, 'Lord, are you going to wash my feet?' Jesus replied, 'You do not realize now what I am doing, but later you will understand.' 'No,' said Peter, 'You shall never wash my feet.' Jesus answered, 'Unless I wash you, you have no part with Me.' 'Then, Lord,' Simon Peter replied, 'not just my feet but my hands and my head as well!' Jesus answered, 'Those who have had a bath need only to wash their feet; their whole body is clean. And you are clean, though not every one of you.' For He knew who was going to betray Him, and that was why He said not every one was clean. When He had finished washing their feet, He put on his clothes and returned to His place. 'Do you understand what I have done for you?' He asked them. 'You call me 'Teacher' and 'Lord,' and rightly so, for that is what I am. Now that I, your Lord and Teacher, have washed your feet, you also should wash one another's feet. I have set you an example that you should do as I have done for you.'" [1]

Have you let Jesus clean your feet?

I believe each of us can experience more security and more peace if we will let Jesus clean our feet. I understand Peter wanting to push Jesus away from his dirty feet. I would feel the same way. I am not worthy for the Lord of the universe to clean my feet. But if we keep pushing Jesus away because we aren't good enough, then we won't have Jesus. We won't ever be good enough. He is holy. We will have to come to grips with the fact that we have dirty feet and by grace, Jesus wants to clean our feet. It's uncomfortable. I don't want Him to touch my dirt, but I can't hide my dirty feet inside of pretty pink socks because He will still be able to smell them.

Recently, at a Christian family camp, I was part of a small group that was really special. When I close my eyes, I can still see the faces of each amazing individual that was a part of the group. Each one embraced an invitation to life-changing intimacy. We all decided to let down our walls and share from our hearts. I believe it was worship. The unity and sweetness there was like a taste of heaven. I wished it would continue, but it ended after only one week.

During our last session together we were asked to pray for the person on our right. My husband was on my right, so I felt fairly comfortable. Then I quickly looked to my left to see who would be praying for me. A young woman in her late twenties and about eight months pregnant sat to my left. Her name was Christelle. She had been the most quiet and reserved one in our group. I quickly concluded I could feel safe. I was therefore not prepared for her prayer. When Christelle's turn to pray came, she said softly, "Jesus, I see you standing before Tiffany offering her Your heart. I pray she will say yes to You and experience the blessing of beholding more of You." It was short and sweet.

I began to cry. I could not dismiss her words; they haunted me all day. Later, when I was in our cabin alone and began to pack, it was as if each item that I held in my hands reminded me of Jesus holding out His heart to me. And as I placed each sweatshirt or sock into a suitcase it seemed so clear to me that although I believed in Jesus and loved Him, I didn't behold Him. I didn't feel worthy enough to really receive His heart. I finally sat down with my journal and drew a picture of Him holding His heart out to me and asking me if I would take it. I wrote out

my honest answer, "No, I'll break it. I don't want
to hurt You!" And then this realization came to
me; I just did. How can I deny Him? I hurt Him
when I refuse Him, even on the premise that I
am not worthy, because He died to make me
worthy.

So finally I said, "Yes, Jesus, I want Your beautiful heart. You are far too trusting of me. Please
help me not to break it. Help me hold it close
to my own and treasure it always." A feeling of
joy blew through me like a gusty autumn wind.

It is an amazing experience to allow Jesus to
touch us. It is a marvelous miracle that He
wants to be so close to us. It is sheer grace that
He is willing to be intimate with us. Religion
appeals to so many people who will worship a
Holy God, but a relationship with Jesus Christ
is a far different deal. We must be willing to let
Him draw near. He wants to wash our feet, and
change our lives. He wants to touch us in a way

that we will be forever changed. He is willing. The more important question is, are You willing? Will you let Jesus wash your feet? Will you surrender your whole soul to Him? Will you trust Him? Are you beyond astounded that He would choose you and trust you? Can you accept His invitation to intimacy?

> There is no dirt on your feet
> That Jesus can't clean!
> There is no stain on your soul
> That Jesus can't cleanse!
> There is no pain in your past
> That He can't redeem!
> Where there's fear of your future,
> Jesus can bring peace.
> Just say yes! Yes! To Jesus
> He can meet your needs!

Let's let Jesus clean our feet!

Jesus' feet

holey feet

8
"Holey" Feet

That is not misspelled. It is different than Holy feet. It is feet with holes in them. It's not a pretty sight. And right now my home smells good, like candles, coffee and fresh-baked cookies. I am having a hard time deciding to sit down and write about the crucifixion. It is gruesome and glorious at the same time. I can't go there without deep emotion. It is a reality that still mystifies me and I wonder how many times I've remembered. How many times have you had communion? Is there anything that I could say that you have not already heard more than a hundred times before? And yet, there is no way to complete a book about Jesus' feet without admiring His piercing. (I have a friend with a sweatshirt that says, "Body piercing saved my life.")

Perhaps you could go pour yourself a glass of red wine and get a slice of bread and have your own personal communion time as you read this chapter. My most meaningful communion experiences have not been during a church service, but rather prolonged quiet times with the Lord either alone or with a few close friends. It is important for us to take time to remember Jesus' extreme love for us.

For years I only had communion at church with little cups of grape juice and tiny crackers served on silver platters that resembled the offering plate. Instead of putting something in the plate, we took something out. It is a good lesson in receiving. I believe that it is hard for us to receive this gift of grace. It isn't hard to eat the crackers and drink the juice. It isn't hard to remember the cross. It is hard to believe that Jesus gave His life to give me righteousness. His death justifies me. Take the word J U S T I F I E D and look at it like this: just as if I'd never sinned.

Do you live forgiven? Do you confess your sin, accept forgiveness and then go the next step and accept what Jesus gives you in its place? For instance, if you confess greed to God and accept the grace given by the blood of Jesus on the cross, do you leave your prayer time changed? Do you see that Jesus' generosity is offered in place of your greed? If you confess fear, do you then take the courage of Christ in its place? Jesus didn't just die for forgiveness of our sins. He died and lives again inside of us. When we die to sin, we must live again for Christ.

He paid the price and by the power of His sacrifice I can be presented blameless in His presence. Jude 1:24-25 says, "To Him who is able to keep you from stumbling and to present you before His glorious presence without fault and with great joy- to the only God our Savior be glory, majesty, power and authority, through Jesus Christ our Lord, before all ages, now and forevermore! Amen." [1] I am blameless before

God but I will never be sinless in this life. There is a significant difference. My sin serves as a daily reminder to me of my need for His power to overcome and His grace to forgive. I can never lose sight of the bloodstained cross. My life is marked by gratitude and worship because by being His child, being blameless cost Him everything!

There's a big difference between getting a gift and receiving a gift. Once, at a speaking engagement, I was surprised to be staying in a beautiful suite. When I entered, I found a gift basket full of treasures. I squealed with delight and began examining them through the cellophane wrapper. There were chocolates, gourmet caramel corn, lotion and bubble bath. When I jumped into the king-sized bed, I smiled as I said my prayers. "Oh thank You, God, for the sweet people who are treating me like a queen. Please bless them back tenfold. Thank You for all these sweet surprises and for spoiling me. I just love being Your little girl!"

Then my mind wandered off, which it tends to do; I remembered that my sister really likes pear-scented lotion. I could give that to her. (Are you honestly shocked, or have you ever done something similar?) I imagined giving my kids all the caramel corn and thought, "Would it be selfish if I kept the chocolate?" I don't remember answering myself. I must have fallen asleep. I couldn't bear to open the basket because it was so beautiful.

After getting home, I told my friend Anne about my blessing basket. She smiled and told me that she loved imagining me being spoiled by my Heavenly Father in that big suite with a bubble bath and eating caramel corn and chocolate in the tub. I laughed and told her that I hadn't opened the basket yet; I was still trying to decide what to do with it. Her smile disappeared quickly and she grabbed my shoulders and marched me to the door. She told me to go home and enjoy how my Father had lavishly loved me! Didn't He know my soul better than I? Didn't He know how to care for me? How horrible to not enjoy His gift!

I hope you have a friend like Anne.

I went home shocked. I hadn't looked at it like that. I remember clearly the crinkling of the cellophane as I opened the basket. It seems so silly, but I really had a hard time opening it. It was so pretty and I thought of so many other people it could bless besides me. I felt selfish, but Anne's anger at my not accepting this gift encouraged me to receive it now.

One of my favorite verses says, "How great is the love the Father has lavished on us, that we should be called children of God! And that is what we are!"[2] It's a truth worth celebrating! The fragrance of the bubbles filled my bathroom. I felt lavishly loved as I leisurely ate the caramel corn and chocolates. I felt supremely spoiled as the warm bubbles surrounded me. Tears of gratitude tumbled down my face. This was grace!

It is not selfish to receive what is given to us. It is as necessary as breathing. We must breathe in to be able to breathe out. If we only do one or the other we will die. Living requires both. How can we give the love of Jesus to others, even our enemies, if we have not first received it?

When we receive all the gifts that Jesus gives us at the cross, how can we ever keep from giving them to others? How can we hold a grudge when we have been forgiven so much? How can we hang onto the pain of our own wounds and act like Jesus just doesn't understand? How much must Jesus' heart have hurt when He hung on the cross, suffering, bleeding, crying out to His Father that He felt forsaken? It must have been the mercy of God in that moment that kept everything ever created from exploding with the grief. Can you hear the sobs of His mother and a few followers?

He was physically abused by being beaten, whipped, and nailed to a cross. He was emotionally abused by the taunting accusations against Him. He was sexually abused by being stripped in public and displayed naked on a cross. He was spiritually abused by being judged by sinners as a fraud, when He was in truth exactly who He said He was. He suffered every form of abuse so that He can comfort us when we are wounded. He is not far-off or distant from our pain. Jesus knows and understands our pain.

Don't you just love Him? I weep with the wonder of who He is and the greatest gift ever given was given to me. How can I ever thank Him enough? This is the best love story ever told for at least two reasons. The first reason is because it is true and the second reason is because we are loved. Can you say that out loud? We are loved! It is our greatest need and it has been met. We are never not loved. When we feel that way we believe lies. God loves us all the time and all the time we are loved beyond our wildest imagination. Would you take a moment of silence now and just let this truth sink in? Soak in the lavish, limitless love of God.

Thank You, Holy God, for forgiving me. Thank You, Holy Spirit, for living inside of me! Thank You, Jesus, for Your Holey feet!

Healed feet

9
Healed Feet

A couple of years ago I had surgery on one of my feet. The surgeon warned me that there are lots of nerve endings in your feet and because feet are so far from your heart, they take a long time to heal. I decided that I wanted to try to recover without pain medication. Why, you ask? Because I had read these verses in Romans, "We rejoice in our sufferings, knowing that suffering produces endurance, and endurance produces character, and character produces hope."[1] Everything listed here appeals to me except the pain. I thought about how Jesus handled suffering. Hebrews 12:2 tells us that "for the joy set before Him, He endured the cross."[2]

I compared it to natural childbirth. I had survived that horrible pain and the beautiful baby at the end seemed so worth it. The pain from the foot surgery was intense. I gritted my teeth and held out as long as I could. After about twenty minutes I couldn't handle it anymore. I started eating the pain medication like candy. I whined and complained about the pain to anyone who would listen. I called people when they stopped coming over to see how I was. They needed to know that I still wasn't better. They needed to pray, probably more for my family than for me.

Before you become totally disgusted with what a baby I was, I have to tell you one more story. A wonderful family from our church came over to bring us a meal while I was healing. Matt works out with my husband Tim. They are strong men. Matt told us when they were over that he had had the same surgery and actually passed out from the pain! Talk about encouragement! Even though I don't have nearly the impressive strength that Matt has, I didn't ever actually pass out.

My foot is healed now. I have a scar that reminds me of that time. The scar will fade some, but it will never go away. This makes sense to me, but when I consider the miracle of Jesus being raised from the dead, I am amazed that He would choose to keep the scars. If I had the power to rise from the dead with a glorious resurrection body, it would be perfect. It certainly wouldn't have scars.

Would you look at Jesus' feet with me as He lives again? In Luke, it says "As they were talking(…)Jesus Himself stood among them, and said to them, 'Peace to you!' But they were startled and frightened and thought that they saw a spirit. And He said to them, 'Why are you troubled, and why do doubts arise in your hearts? See My hands and My feet, that it is I Myself. Touch Me, and see. For a spirit does not have flesh and bones as you see that I have.' And when He said this, He showed them His hands and His feet. And while they still disbelieved for joy and were marveling, He said to them, 'Have you anything here to eat?'" [3]

I'm having trouble writing about this right now. My eyes are filled with tears and my chin is quivering. I want to write, but I think that it's difficult because I am filled with joy and marveling at the beauty of Jesus. Can you even believe that He came to find them, and showed them the scars that He had from suffering the most horrible, gruesome death in their place just days before? And after being beaten for their sins and killed, He says "Touch Me."[4] He invites them to touch Him; Holy God in flesh who has risen from the dead! I just love how Jesus loves us.

Oh, Sweet Savior! I love You. How can it be that You would suffer and die for me? How amazed I am that You gave Your life and shed Your blood to set me free from my sin and damnation! It was my sin that caused You so much pain and then

You come to me and ask me touch You. And, oh, how I want to touch You. I want to touch Your beautiful face so tenderly and look into Your eyes and say thank You! I want to tell You that I love You. I want to wash Your scarred feet with my tears of worship and gratitude. I want to serve You. I want to be with You. I want to know You more and more. Thank You for the invitation! Thank You for the opportunity! And about this book Lord Jesus, I am sorry that I have dreaded working on it. I want it to be more than obedience. I want it to be worship to You. Please anoint every word and multiply every effort to feed Your sheep. Please take these loaves and fishes, this paper and ink, and bless it. You are the miracle maker, the blesser, and the provider of all that we need. You are beautiful beyond description, too incredible for words. Who can fathom Your infinite wisdom? Who can grasp the heights of Your love? We are blessed more than we can comprehend, and are at a loss as to how we can appreciate all that You've done for us.

This is one of those rare moments in life where I just don't have words to fill the space. This is a miracle in itself. I don't want to cloud this all up with words. Let's leave the next two pages blank for worship. Either you can put your own thoughts down or just leave them blank as a time of silence.

Jesus' feet

Would you mind reading this passage one more time? "And when He said this, He showed them His hands and His feet." [4] What would it be like to offer the ones that hurt you a look at your scars? Do you think you could do it? The two typical responses to being hurt are to fight or to flee. We either want to hit back and have revenge, or we want to run away and avoid the ones that hurt us. Here is Jesus blowing our minds again by coming to the disciples and being vulnerable, forgiving them for all their sins that caused Him so much pain, and so soon after!

He says "Behold, I have engraved you on the palms of my hands." [5] Think about the scars on His hands and feet. These are places that you would see every day. So many scars are hidden. My Dad had open heart surgery a few years ago and healed so well that I forgot he had it done. Last summer, when I was visiting he came out of his bedroom with his shirt off and his scar surprised me. It isn't something that I see very often. But we see our hands and feet every day as we put on our shoes and as we play or we work or cook or eat. God wants us to know that He remembers. He chooses to remember. He will not forget. He has promised us that.

And speaking of cooking and eating, how cool is it that Jesus asks them for something to eat? Isn't He great? It is the absolute best party of all time, right? And yet nobody has said anything about food. Jesus says, "Where's the food? This is a party, isn't it?" I didn't put that quote in red, because it's sort of my paraphrase. They gave Him a boiled fish. Yuck! They should have given Him chocolate!

What would you like to give Jesus? We know that He gave us everything and will never forget us because He bears the scars on His hands and healed feet.

10

Jesus' Feet

Well, this is the final chapter of the book. It has taken me about two years to get here. I hope that it hasn't taken you that long to read it. And I want to thank you for reading this book, because that makes all the time and effort worth it. It has been my prayer that you have been blessed by Jesus' feet.

I would like to end by listening to the final words that Jesus spoke before His feet left the earth to ascend into heaven. "Then Jesus came to them and said, 'All authority in heaven and on earth has been given to Me. Therefore go and make disciples of all nations, baptizing them in the name of the Father and of the Son and of the Holy Spirit, and teaching them to obey everything I have commanded you.

And surely I am with you always, to the very end of the age.'" [1]

Taking these verses apart is interesting to me. Jesus tells us that all authority is given to Him and then gives us a command. How often do I look at His commands as suggestions or invitations that I can choose to accept or decline? A more accurate account would be that Jesus commands and I either obey or disobey. I want to repent. I want to always obey. I want to believe in His authority and follow His example. He will never ask me to do something that He has not already done or that He won't be able to enable me to do.

If I follow in His holy footsteps, I will have Jesus' feet. They were once trusting, tiny feet like His. They have been and will be humble, dirty feet when they are obedient feet. And let's not forget that Jesus doesn't just ask us to sacrifice when we follow His footsteps. He also asks us to dance. He delights in us and woos us. Our lives with Jesus will look like a romance. He will also show us how the abundant life is filled with adventures like walking on water so that we will have wet feet. When we spend all this time with Jesus, we will begin to look like Him and sinners will feel safe with us, safe enough to come to us and know that we will offer them grace. They will share their sorrows and their tears with us and we will have the privilege of telling them about Jesus.

When we get close enough to Jesus to see His holey feet and how He chose to keep the scars even when His feet were healed, and we believe He is who He says He is, the Savior of the World, and we are baptized in His Holy Name, then we will have clean feet.

Jesus wants the cry of our hearts to be His hands and feet. He loved and trusted His Father so much that this was the cry of His heart.

Jesus came to earth to be an example of how faith is walked out. The last part of the great commission is that Jesus is with us always even to the very end of the age, but then Jesus "was taken up into heaven and sat down at the right hand of God." [2] So how can He be with us always? How can we do the things that Jesus did?

In Luke, He says, "And now I will send the Holy Spirit, just as My Father promised. But stay here in the city until the Holy Spirit comes and fills you with power from heaven." [3]

Of course I don't know your church background, but I just want to say that I have not heard very much teaching about the Holy Spirit. I heard all about God's creation of the earth and how He spoke through a burning bush and delivered His people from slavery. I heard all about Jesus and how He was born to the Virgin

Mary and all about His miracles and His death
on the cross for my sins. But I have heard much
less about the Holy Spirit.

When I consider the Trinity, it seems that I
know far less about the third part that is supposed to be living within me. Maybe that's why
I don't feel the power to do the very things that
Jesus did. It was my New Year's resolution this
year to be drunk in the Spirit. Ephesians 5:18
says, "Don't be drunk with wine, because that
will ruin your life. Instead, be filled with the
Holy Spirit." [4] When I think about people drunk
with wine, I mostly imagine laughter and freedom. The effects of the wine cause us to lose
our inhibitions.

When I had the privilege of going to Sierra
Leone, Africa, I saw the people there dance as
they worshipped with an abandonment that
I had never seen before. I felt very white and

uptight. I was disappointed that I had not seen this modeled for me as a child or been encouraged to experience worship in this beautiful way. I felt that now as an adult, I would not ever be able to abandon myself to dancing like that. It was so soft and subtle that I doubted it at first, but I believe I heard the Alpha and Omega laughing at my conclusions. He reminded me that He is eternal and that I am always His child. He asked me to dance, to just close my eyes and quit thinking about anybody else but Him. He asked me to listen to the song that He sings over me and dance. I did. And I didn't hear anyone else laughing.

We can be sure that the Spirit of God is inside us, and that we can stop doubting that this voice of God will direct and guide us. When we stop second-guessing all the time and start to trust more, we will lose some of those inhibitions. We will experience freedom!

What has the Spirit been whispering to you?
What crazy kind of mission does God want you
to go on? How has He asked you specifically
to be Jesus' feet? It might not be the same as
what was asked of me. He asked me to write
a book. I wrestled and whined and thought of
every excuse I could, but the desire to be all
that He created me to be was too strong. I was
grieving the Spirit inside me by disobeying the
prompting.

To walk like Jesus walked and follow in His
footsteps, we must see what mattered most to
Him. It is His Spirit He has given us to guide
us. We must open our eyes to see the hurting
around us and to care. We must do what Jesus
did. We must open the eyes of the blind; we
must set the captives free from their bondage.
We must feed the poor.

Since you have spent time at Jesus' feet, you have
chosen what cannot be taken from you, and you

can give that gift to others. Look around you; look at the world on which you are revolving. Is there someone with whom you can share the glorious gifts given to you?

Jesus said, "From everyone who has been given much, much will be demanded. And from the one trusted with much, much more will be expected." [5] We have been given much, more than we can even conceive. God has been abundantly good to us. He has loved us with an everlasting love. He has forgiven us all our sins. He has promised us salvation, redemption, and heaven. We are truly blessed. Let our lives look like Psalm 116:12: "What can I give back to God for the blessings He's poured out on me?" [6]

The words of Jesus in Matthew 25 motivate me to see beyond myself and my own needs. "For I was hungry and you gave Me something to eat, I was thirsty and you gave Me something to drink, I was a stranger and you invited Me in, I needed clothes and you clothed Me, I was sick and you looked after Me, I was in prison and you came to visit Me."[7] Have you seen the hungry and thirsty? They are all around us. There are so many different kinds of hunger. The reality is that there is enough food in this world to feed everyone and that every day people die of starvation. This shouldn't happen. We have been given much and we need to share it.

There is also a hunger of the soul. We are surrounded every day by those who are hungry for peace, love, healing, and hope. In a nutshell, the world is hungry for Jesus! Do we look others in the eye knowing that this is where our God has chosen to be visible? This is His image. Will we see the deeper destiny of our lives to be the very hands and feet of Jesus? Will we reach out to others and offer all that we have been given?

Mother Teresa looked for, and found, Jesus in the poorest of the poor. She also knew that His presence was within her. She had His compassion to offer. I have this beautiful shiny silver angel hanging in my kitchen with a quote from Mother Teresa. It says, "We can not do great things, only small things with great love."

"As it is written, 'How beautiful are the feet of those who bring good news!'"[8] With the Holy Spirit inside of us and the example of Jesus before us, I pray that we will embrace the call to be Jesus' Feet!

Compassion International is an incredible organization that feeds the poor in Jesus' name. Our family sponsors two children through them. Samantha lives in the Philippines and I have not met her yet. Jean lives in Haiti and I had the incredible privilege of meeting him. He is an orphan who lives with his two sisters in his Aunt and Uncle's home. Through Compassion International, I am able to send him to school to learn to read and write and possibly break the chain of poverty for him. He is fed and learns about Jesus. It costs us $38 each month. He also received medical care recently when he fell out of a tree and broke his arm.

We began sponsoring Jean when he was six years old. My daughter and I were able to meet him when he was eleven years old.

We had exchanged letters and pictures with him for five years. We recognized each other right away. We hugged and cried. He speaks a different language, so we had an interpreter who helped us to communicate. I told him that I had saved all his letters and pictures and then waited for the interpreter to tell him what I said. Then I heard him laugh and speak to the interpreter while I waited to see what was so funny to him. He told me that he had also saved all my letters and pictures. We are very much the same. Our skins are different in color, and our lifestyles are worlds apart, but we both treasure the people that God has brought into our lives.

I would like to encourage you to sponsor a child through Compassion International. It has been a big blessing in my life and I know that it has been a blessing to the children we sponsor as well as their families.

Please visit
www.Compassion.com/tiffanyleethompson
to sponsor a child today!

About the Author

Tiffany Lee Thompson loves her Papa, His Son and His Spirit. She is excited about falling more and more in love with this Trinity!

A native of the Midwest, Tiffany and her husband of twenty-five years, Timothy, live in Wisconsin; she adores him and the five children who have joined their family because of love. Some of her favorites are flowers, friends, eating chocolate and talking – but cooking, not so much. You would rather have her tell you a story than cook you dinner! She is named after her Grandfather, Lester Lee, who owned a newspaper, and his daughter, Dinah Lee, who shares her wisdom through counseling. They are both beautiful people who have used words to bless others, and if you met them first, you would want to meet Tiffany Lee.

A vibrant, colorful woman with many words, Tiffany always got into trouble at school for talking in class – but she actually found a job where she gets paid for talking! She has been an international public speaker for over twenty years and has visited twenty different countries. This is her first book, in response to requests from many listeners for even more words.

If you're a "wordaholic," like Tiffany, you may even want to check out her website at:

www.tiffanyleethompson.com

Sources

Introduction letter

1. Luke 10:38-42. The Holy Bible: New Century Version, copyright 1987, 1988, 1991 by Word Publishing.

Chapter 1

1. Isaiah 66:1. Scripture taken from The Holy Bible: New International Version, copyright 1973, 1978, 1984 by International Bible Society. Used by permission of Zondervan. All rights reserved.

Chapter 2

1. Luke 4:2 NIV
2. 1 John 4:16 NIV
3. John 2:5 NIV
4. Revelation 1:15 NIV
5. Psalm 46:10 NIV

6. Psalm 46:10. Scripture taken from New American Standard Bible, copyright 1960, 1962, 1963, 1968, 1971, 1972, 1973, 1975, 1977, by The Lockman Foundation. Used by permission.

7. Psalm 46:10 NCV

8. Psalm 46:10. Scripture taken from The Message, copyright 1993, 1994, 1995, 1996, 2000, 2001, 2002. Used by permission of NavPress Publishing Group.

9. Matthew 25:23. Scripture quotations are from The Holy Bible: English Standard Version, copyright 2001 by Crossway Bibles, a publishing ministry of Good News Publishers. Used by permission. All rights reserved.

Chapter 3

1. Zephaniah 3:17 NIV
2. John 2:9-11 NAS
3. Ephesians 5:18 NCV
4. Luke 7:33-34 NCV

Chapter 4

1. John 6:38 The Message.
2. Hebrews 1:3 NIV
3. James 5:16 NIV

Chapter 5

1. Matthew 14:22-31 NIV
2. <u>If You Want to Walk on Water You've Got to Get Out of the Boat</u>, copyright 2001 by John Ortberg, Zondervan Publishing. Page 28.
3. Galatians 1:10 NCV
4. Romans 12:18 NAS
5. Ecclesiastes 4:9-11 NAS

Chapter 6

1. Luke 7:36-50 NIV
2. John 9:5 NIV
3. Matthew 5:14 NIV
4. Psalm 56:8 ESV
5. John 8:32 NIV

6. Romans 8:26 NIV

Chapter 7

1. John 13:5-15 NIV

Chapter 8

1. Jude 1:24-25 NIV
2. 1 John 3:1 NIV

Chapter 9

1. Romans 5:3-4 ESV
2. Hebrews 12:2 NIV
3. Luke 24:36-41 ESV
4. Luke 24:39 NIV
5. Isaiah 49:16 ESV

Chapter 10

1. Matthew 28:18–20 NIV
2. Mark 16:19 ESV
3. Luke 24:49 Scripture taken from the Holy Bible: New Living Translation, copyright 1996 by Tyndale House Foundation.

4. Ephesians 5:18 NLT
5. Luke 12:48 NCV
6. Psalm 116:12 The Message
7. Matthew 25:35-36 NIV
8. Romans 10:15 NIV

Made in the USA
San Bernardino, CA
15 January 2016